A WHOLE WORLD OF
BIRDS

ANNA CLAYBOURNE AND YEKYUNG KWON

FRANKLIN
WATTS

First published in Great Britain in 2024 by Franklin Watts
Copyright © Hodder and Stoughton, 2024

Commissioning editor: Grace Glendinning
Designer: Lisa Peacock
Consultant: Dr Ashley Ward, professor of animal behaviour
at the University of Sydney

HB ISBN: 978 1 4451 8849 2
PB ISBN: 978 14451 8850 8
EB ISBN: 978 14451 8848 3

Printed and bound in Dubai

Franklin Watts, an imprint of
Hachette Children's Group
Part of Hodder and Stoughton
Carmelite House
50 Victoria Embankment
London EC4Y 0DZ
An Hachette UK Company

www.hachette.co.uk
www.hachettechildrens.co.uk

The authorised representative in the EEA is Hachette Ireland,
8 Castlecourt Centre, Castleknock Road, Castleknock,
Dublin 15, D15 YF6A, Ireland

MIX
Paper | Supporting
responsible forestry
FSC® C104740
FSC
www.fsc.org

The website addresses (URLs) included in this book were valid at
the time of going to press. However, it is possible that contents or
addresses may have changed since the publication of this book. No
responsibility for any such changes can be accepted by either the
author or the Publisher.

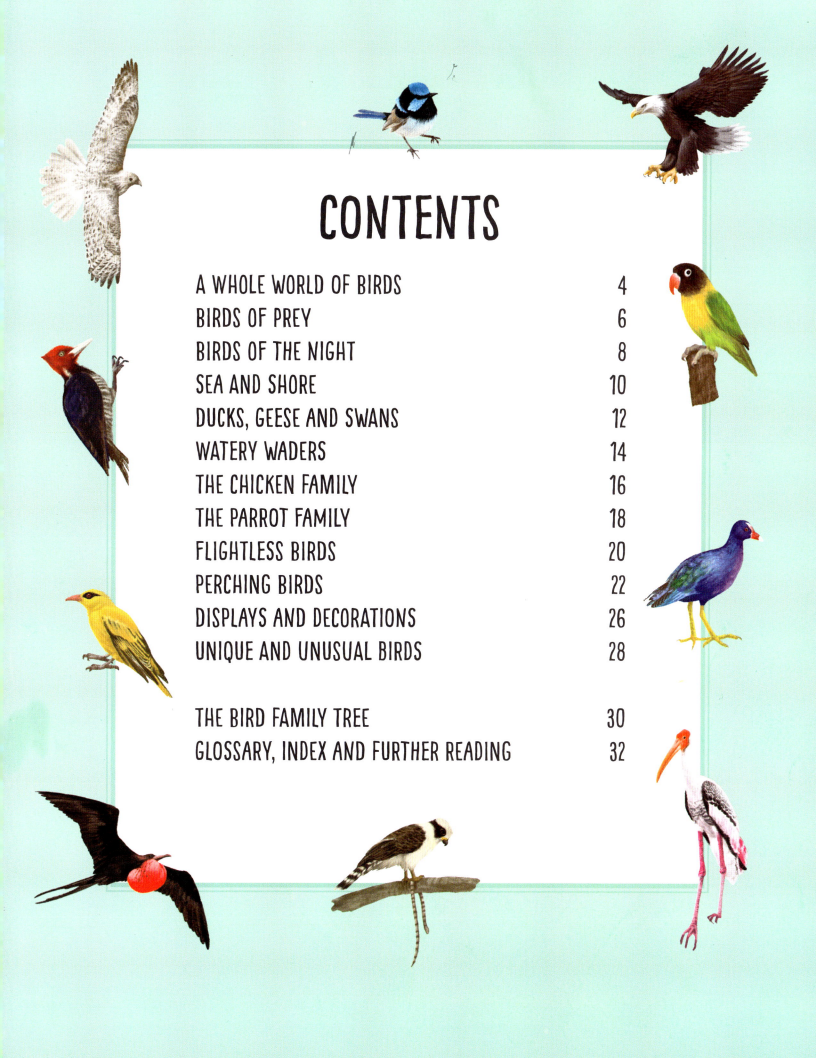

CONTENTS

A WHOLE WORLD OF BIRDS

Wherever you live – in a city, the countryside, or by the sea – you'll probably see birds every day.

Canada goose

WHAT ARE BIRDS?

We all know a bird when we see one! That's because birds are unlike any other kind of animal. They're the only living animals with feathers. They all have wings, though they can't all fly. And they walk on two legs, like us!

SQUAWK!

Beak

Feathers

Two wings

Two legs

Birds' feet look similar to some dinosaurs' feet.

All birds hatch from eggs.

Northern cardinals visit gardens and bird feeders in North America.

The rare St Lucia parrot is only found on the Caribbean island of St Lucia.

You can find a blue-footed booby on the shores of the Galapagos Islands, and other coasts nearby.

WHERE DID THEY COME FROM?

Birds came from dinosaurs! Some dinosaurs had feathers, and some feathered dinosaurs gradually evolved (changed over many generations) into flying birds. Birds are the closest living relatives of dinosaurs.

The Antarctic is the home of the amazing Emperor penguin.

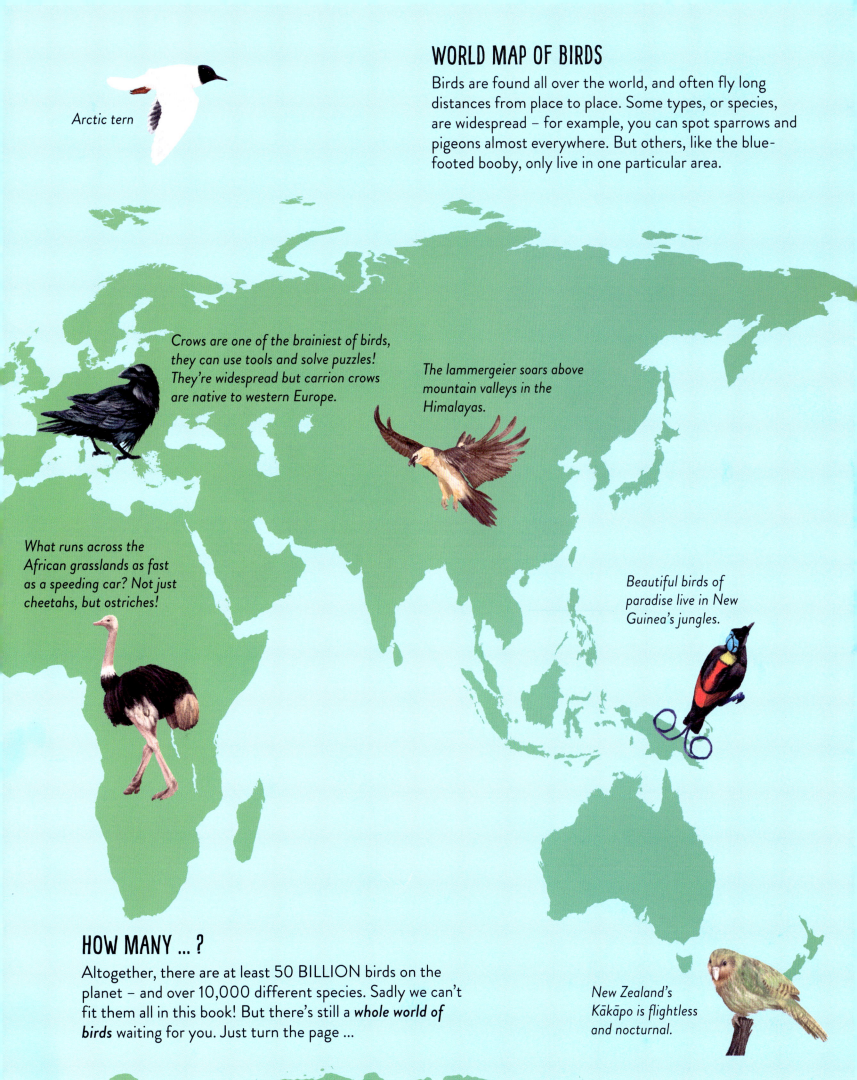

WORLD MAP OF BIRDS

Birds are found all over the world, and often fly long distances from place to place. Some types, or species, are widespread – for example, you can spot sparrows and pigeons almost everywhere. But others, like the blue-footed booby, only live in one particular area.

Arctic tern

Crows are one of the brainiest of birds, they can use tools and solve puzzles! They're widespread but carrion crows are native to western Europe.

The lammergeier soars above mountain valleys in the Himalayas.

What runs across the African grasslands as fast as a speeding car? Not just cheetahs, but ostriches!

Beautiful birds of paradise live in New Guinea's jungles.

HOW MANY ... ?

Altogether, there are at least 50 BILLION birds on the planet – and over 10,000 different species. Sadly we can't fit them all in this book! But there's still a *whole world of birds* waiting for you. Just turn the page ...

New Zealand's Kākāpo is flightless and nocturnal.

BIRDS OF PREY

Birds of prey are strong, fast hunting birds. They swoop down on their dinner and grab it with their sharp talons and beaks.

Golden eagle

It's not actually bald – it just has a white head!

Bald eagle

MIGHTY EAGLES

The eagles include the biggest birds of prey. Some are so large and strong they can hunt monkeys, sheep or even deer.

Tufty head feathers look like a crown.

Harpy eagle

Booted eagle

African fish eagle

Andean condor

One of the world's biggest birds, with a wingspan of up to 3.3 m.

VULTURES

Vultures are birds of prey, but instead of hunting, they mostly eat carrion – the leaftovers of animals that have already died.

However, vultures don't circle around in the sky waiting for things to die – that's a myth! They just fly around to search for food.

Many vultures ARE really bald! Scientists think this helps them to cool down.

Griffon vulture

Changeable hawk-eagle

Lammergeier, or bearded vulture

Lesser yellow-headed vulture

Martial eagle

FALCONS AND HAWKS

These birds of prey are usually smaller, but they're still fierce hunters. What they eat depends on their size – other birds, mice, lizards and frogs, fish, rabbits, insects or even snakes.

Osprey, or fish hawk

Peregrine falcon

The fastest bird in the world – it can swoop down from the sky at 320 km/h!

Gyrfalcon

Chinese sparrowhawk

Pale chanting goshawk

New Zealand falcon

Australian hobby

Pygmy falcon

Crested honey buzzard

Feeds on bees and honey! It has a special groove in its tongue to help it slurp the honey up.

Laughing falcon, or snake hawk

Red-legged seriema

Not scared of deadly snakes!

7

BIRDS OF THE NIGHT

Most birds are active in the daytime, but owls, and some other birds, are nocturnal and prefer the night.

AMAZING OWLS

Owls are birds of prey, but look different from their cousins the eagles and hawks. They have big, round faces, which act like a satellite dish to bounce sounds into their ears.

You can't see their ears, as they're hidden under their feathers. But owls have very good hearing to help them hunt in the dark.

The smallest owl, only 15 cm tall – that's about the same size as a toothbrush!

Elf owl

Jungle owlet

Burrowing owl

Round dish-shaped face, or 'facial disk'.

Barn owl

Northern boobook

Fish owl

Eastern screech owl

Tawny owls really do say 'tu-whit, tu-woo', but it takes two! A female calls 'tu-whit', and a male answers 'tu-woo'.

These are not actually horns or ears, just feathery tufts.

Long-eared owl

Great horned owl

Madagascar-scops owl

Snowy owl

Tawny owl

Fluffy feathers muffle the owl's wings, so prey animals don't hear it coming.

Great grey owl

Ears are here.

Little owl

WE LOVE THE NIGHT, TOO!
Besides owls, several other types of birds are awake at night. Nocturnal birds often sing in the dark to let each other know where they are – sometimes keeping us awake, too.

Famous for its beautiful, musical night-time song.

Lyre-tailed nightjar

Calls at night, making a noisy buzzing sound.

Corncrake

Common nightingale

Northern mockingbird

Eastern whip-poor-will

This large water bird makes a spooky hooting sound at night, a bit like a wolf howling.

Common loon

Black-crowned night heron

European robin

Often sings in the day AND stays up late at night!

North island brown kiwi

Eurasian nightjar

SEA AND SHORE

Seabirds live by the sea, where they can dive into the water to catch fish, or hunt for worms, clams or oysters on the shore.

FISHING BIRDS

These seabirds catch their food from the water, by diving, swooping or swimming. When they're not out at sea hunting, they often nest on rocky ledges on seaside cliffs and crags.

Herring gull

Little gull

Black noddy

Whiskered auklet

Arctic tern

Ashy storm petrel

Noddies fly low over the sea and scoop up fish and squid.

Black guillemot

Gannet

Gannets and guillemots dive down from the sky and plunge underwater to catch fish.

Wandering albatross

Atlantic puffin

The wandering albatross has the longest wingspan of any bird, up to 3.7 m.

Brown pelican

SHOREBIRDS

Shorebirds find their food on the shore or in the shallows. Some have long beaks for digging up worms and shellfish from the sand and mud, or long legs for wading in the water.

Pied avocet

Pied oystercatcher

Red knot

Little stint

Pied means two-coloured or multicoloured.

Sanderling

Red-necked phalarope

Red-legged cormorant

Greater yellowlegs

Pacific golden plover

Shy mollymawk

Black stilt

Surfbird

Northern fulmar

Surfbirds hunt for food among the crashing waves.

DUCKS, GEESE AND SWANS

These water birds swim on the water surface, like living boats. They're found on rivers, ponds, lakes and canals, or sometimes in the sea.

DUCKS

Ducks are the smallest birds in their family, and come in a huge range of colours and patterns. Often, the male is more colourful, while the female is camouflaged.

Australian freckled duck

female

Hooded merganser

male

Mallard

Mandarin duck

Torrent duck

Pacific black duck

Steamer sucks are huge, heavy sea ducks that can't fly. They use their short wings to paddle themselves along like a paddle steamer!

Fuegian steamer duck

African pygmy goose (Actually a duck!)

Indian runner duck

Some ducks are farm animals and are bred and kept for their eggs, feathers or meat.

Radjah shelduck

Rosy-billed pochard

West Indian whistling duck

The colour 'teal' is named after the stripe on this duck's head!

Eurasian teal

HIGH FLYERS

Geese are somewhere between a duck and a swan, with a medium-long neck. Many species migrate long distances to spend the summer and the winter in different places.

Canada goose

Bar-headed geese fly incredibly high on their migrations across the Himalayas – more then 8,000 m up in the air!

Bar-headed goose

Emden goose

The large, fierce and very clever Emden goose is sometimes used as a guard animal to chase away intruders.

SERENE SWANS

Amazingly big and beautiful with their long, slender necks and folded wings, swans are instantly recognisable.

Mute swan

You usually see swans swimming, but they can fly, too.

Get their names from their loud, hooting calls.

Black swan

Whooper swan

WATERY WADERS

These birds wade in watery marshes, swamps, streams, rivers, ponds and the shallow edges of lakes.

Has a gap in its beak, even when it's shut!

African openbill

LEGS FOR PADDLING

Wading birds come from many different birds familes, but they usually have long, skinny legs without feathers, to make it easier to wade and paddle. They mainly eat small water animals like worms, snails, tiny fish, shrimps and water insects.

Eurasian coot

Painted stork

Jabiru

Black-crowned crane

American purple gallinule

Anhinga

Anhingas and darters can spring or 'dart' their long snaky necks forward suddenly to grab fish from the water.

Coots have huge feet with wide flaps on them. They use them to swim, and to walk on mud, marshy ground or reedy river banks.

Giant coot

African darter

Australasian darter

Black heron

Grey heron

Zigzag heron

Titicaca grebe

This cunning heron uses its wings to make a shady cover over the water. Fish swim into it thinking they've found a hiding place, and get snapped up.

Madagascar grebe

Great crested grebe

Spoonbills wade along in shallow water and sweep their spoon-shaped beaks from side to side to catch small fish and shrimps.

American bittern

Pheasant-tailed jacana

Jacanas build their nests on floating lake plants. They have very long toes to help them walk on water plants without sinking.

Roseate spoonbill

African jacana

FLAMBOYANT FLAMINGOS

Tall and bright pink, with very long legs and huge beaks, you can't miss a flamingo! Some live on coasts, but others wade in lakes.

Chilean flamingo

Andean flamingo

Flamingos feed by sticking their beaks into the water or mud upside-down to catch tiny shrimps. The shrimps are what make the flamingos pink!

THE CHICKEN FAMILY

Cluck cluck! When you think of a chicken, you probably think of an egg-laying farm animal. But chickens and their relatives are actually part of a big bird family.

A tame version of the red junglefowl from eastern Asia

GROUND DWELLERS

These birds often live on the ground, in forests or grasslands. They peck and forage for insects, small lizards, seeds, roots or shoots to eat.

Sri Lankan junglefowl

Yellow-knobbed curassow

Helmeted curassow

Malayan crested argus

Yellow-necked spurfowl

Domestic or farm chicken

Helmeted guineafowl

Common pheasant

Many of these birds can't fly far – they often run instead. But they may fly up into a tree to roost, or rest, for the night.

Blue eared pheasant

A stunningly beautiful chicken relative, the male has layers of long, speckled feathers dotting with bright blue spots.

Palawan peacock-pheasant

Common quail

Quails are very small chicken relatives

Malayan peacock-pheasant

HUNTED FOR FOOD

Wild chickens, turkeys and their relatives, especially grouse and pheasants, often get hunted for food by other animals, such as foxes, cougars and bears – and sometimes by humans too. Many of them have great camouflage to help them hide in their moorland or forest homes.

Domestic turkey

Greater sage grouse

Occellated turkey

A tame version of the South Mexican wild turkey

Chinese grouse

Greater prairie chicken

Caucasian black grouse

The willow ptarmigan grows white feathers for the winter, to blend in with the snow.

Willow ptarmigan

Willow ptarmigan

Australian brushturkey

Tongan megapode

These turkey relatives are called megapodes, meaning 'big feet'.

17

THE PARROT FAMILY

Parrots are beautiful, noisy and incredibly clever birds. They come in many shapes, sizes and colours.

Biggest parrot, sometimes growing to over 1 m long.

Hyacinth macaw

Scarlet macaw

St Lucia parrot

PERCHING PARROTS

Most parrots have curved claws for perching on branches, and big, strong beaks that they use to crack open nuts and seeds. They mainly live in tropical forests, where they nest in hollows in trees. You'll often see bright flashes of colour when parrots fly overhead.

Orange-cheeked parrot

Though most parrots live in warm tropical places, a few species, such as rose-ringed parakeets, have spread out around the world, and often live in cities.

Rose-ringed parakeet

Black-headed parrot

Eleonora cockatoo

Rainbow lorikeet

Turquoise parrot

Violet-necked lory

Palm cockatoo

Famous for its ability to dance to music

Major Mitchell's cockatoo

Kea

Two unusual parrots from New Zealand

New Zealand kākā

MINI PARROTS!

Parrots can be pretty big, like hyancinth and scarlet macaws – but some are teeny!

Buff-faced pygmy parrot

Smallest parrot, just 8 cm long.

Rosy-faced lovebird

Yellow-collared lovebird

Fischer's lovebird pair

Lovebirds get their name because a male and a female become partners for life, and pine for each other when they're not together.

PRETTY POLLY!

Can parrots really talk? Yes! Many parrot species are very good at mimicking, or copying, the sounds they hear, including human speech. But some smart parrots also seem to learn to use words like we do, they say what's on their mind!

Bourke's parakeet

Budgerigars are brilliant talkers. One budgie named Puck learned 1,728 words!

A famous African grey parrot called Alex would chat to his owner and could name colours, shapes and foods when he saw them.

African grey parrot

Budgerigar, or budgie

FLIGHTLESS BIRDS

All birds have wings, but not all birds can fly!

The biggest bird on the planet, it can stand up to 2.8 m tall, weigh 160 kg and run at 70 km/h.

FAST RUNNERS

If you can't fly away from danger, you need anopther way to escape. These flightless birds are big and tall, with strong legs for running fast. If that doesn't work, they may use their large claws to kick their enemies!

Southern cassowary

Common ostrich

Emu

Extra large, sharp claw on inner toe

The flightless cormorant is only found on the Galapagos Islands. It looks like other cormorants, but can't fly.

Flightless cormorant

KIWIS AND KĀKĀPŌS

Several famous flightless birds come from New Zealand. They include kiwis and kākāpōs, which hide from danger by nesting in burrows.

Okarito kiwi

Great spotted kiwi

South Island takahē

Kākāpō, a large, flightless parrot

Weka

These two birds hide their nests under thick bushes.

20

PENGUINS

Penguins are probably the most famous of all flightless birds. They live in the southern hemisphere, mainly in cold, icy places.

On land or on ice, penguins waddle or slide around. In the sea, they use their wings like flippers to swim and steer at high speed.

About 1 m tall.

Emperor penguin

King penguin

Adelie penguin

Cool crest!

Northern rockhopper penguin

The fastest-swimming penguin, it can zoom along at 35 km/h.

Gentoo penguin

Chinstrap penguin

Only around 30 cm tall

Little blue penguin

Waitaha penguin

Macaroni penguin

African penguin

PERCHING BIRDS

Think of the small, familiar birds you see in gardens, parks and cities, such as sparrows, robins, blackbirds and crows. They are the perching birds, or passerines.

PERCHING EVERYWHERE!

The perching birds are a huge bird family – in fact they make up more than half of all bird species. They're found all over the world, and if you see a wild bird, it's probably a passerine.

Black-faced cuckooshrike

European robin

Superb fairywren

White-crested laughingthrush

African golden oriole

Australian logrunner

You can tell a perching bird from other birds by its perching feet.

Three toes at the front

One at the back

Helmet vanga

Indian paradise flycatcher

Bronzed drongo

White-throated treecreeper

Red-billed leiothrix

FABULOUS FEATHERS

Some birds have such bright feathers, colourful crests or amazing tails, it can be hard to believe they're real.

Gouldian finch

Galah cockatoo

Himalayan monal

Violet-backed starling

Iridescent feathers seem to sparkle and change colour as the bird moves.

Spangled coquette

King of saxony bird of paradise

Turquoise-browed motmot

Indian paradise flycatcher

Wilson's bird of paradise

Marvellous spatuletail

Ribbon tailed astrapia

This astrapia has the longest tail of any bird, compared to its body size.

Amazing tails!

Andean cock-of-the-rock

Superb lyrebird

The superb lyrebird can mimic any noise it hears in its surroundings, such as other bird songs as well as chainsaws and dog barks.

UNIQUE AND UNUSUAL BIRDS

Some of these unique birds are unusual-looking,
while others do some very unusual things ...

Secretary bird

Shoebill

Clacks its big bill to
make a rattling sound.

Toco toucan

Uses its huge beak to
reach into tree holes
to find food.

Huge staring eyes!

Great potoo

A long-legged bird of prey
that walks around on the
ground to hunt insects,
lizards and snakes.

Marabou stork

Big dangly wattle,
or throat flap.

Sri Lanka frogmouth

Common cuckoo

Southern bald ibis

Cuckoos lay their eggs in
other birds' nests, so that the
other mother bird feeds and
cares for their babies.

Magnificent frigatebird

Helmeted hornbill

The world's smallest bird at just 5-6 cm long, it's similar in size to the world's biggest bees and wasps.

Bee hummingbird

The hoatzin is famous for its stinky smell! It also escapes from danger by falling into water and swimming away.

Hoatzin

The male inflates a huge balloon of bright red skin on his neck to attract a female.

Sword-billed hummingbird

The only bird whose beak is longer than its body!

This little bird really is a vampire! When it's hungry it will peck other birds, such as the blue-footed booby, and slurp up their blood.

Vampire finch

Long-wattled umbrellabird

Australian pelican

The longest beak of all, at up to 50 cm long. Pelicans have big stretchy pouches under their beaks, which they fill with fish when hunting.

Danger – keep away from this bird! Its feathers and skin contain a deadly poison to put off predators.

Hooded pitohui

Moustache

Inca tern

Can beat its wings at up to 200 times per SECOND! This makes it buzz like a flying insect.

Ruby-throated hummingbird

THE BIRD FAMILY TREE

Which type of bird is which, and how are they all related?
This bird family tree lets you see all the different groups of birds at a glance.

Chickens and pheasants

Grouse

Cranes

Parrots

Loons and grebes

Ducks, geese and swans

Herons

Cormorants

Emus

Ostriches

Cassowaries

Kiwis

Hawks

Falcons

Eagles

Owls

Wrens

Sparrows

Thrushes

Finches

Starlings

Pigeons

Crows

Kingfishers

Woodpeckers

Gulls and terns

Hummingbirds

Oystercatchers

Storks

Albatrosses

GLOSSARY

Antarctic The large, icy continent or land mass around the South Pole.

Bill Another word for a bird's beak.

Bird of prey A bird that hunts and eats other animals.

Camouflage Patterns and colours that help an animal to hide by blending in with its surroundings.

Carrion Animals that have already died, which some birds (and other animals) like to eat.

Domestic Animals that are bred to be pets or farm animals, instead of being wild.

Evolve Living things evolve when they gradually change over many generations.

Generation The life of a living thing, from when it is born to when it has its own babies.

Himalayas The world's biggest mountain range, which is in the middle of Asia.

Iridescent Bright and shiny, and seeming to change colour when seen from different angles.

Mimic To imitate or copy the sound or appearance of another animal or thing.

Nocturnal Active at night.

Ocellated Covered in spots that look similar to eyes.

Passerine A common type of bird, usually quite small, with feet shaped for perching.

Pied Patterned in two different colours.

Predator An animal that hunts and eats other animals.

Prey An animal that gets hunted and eaten by other animals.

Roost Birds roost when they settle down in a tree or other safe place to rest.

Species The scientific name for a particular type of living thing.

Territory The area that a bird (or other animal) guards and defends as its own.

Wattle A fold or flap of skin that some birds have on their throats.

Wingspan The measurement between a birds' two wingtips when its wings are fully spread out.

INDEX

FURTHER READING

The Big Book of Birds
By Yuval Zommer (Thames & Hudson, 2019)

The Children's Book of Birdwatching: Nature-Friendly Tips for Spotting Birds
By Dan Rouse (Dorling Kindersley, 2023)